MODERN-DAY STRATEGIES FOR COMMUNITY ENGAGEMENT

MODERN-DAY STRATEGIES FOR COMMUNITY ENGAGEMENT

HOW TO EFFECTIVELY BUILD BRIDGES BETWEEN PEOPLE AND THE BOTTOM LINE

MAKARA RUMLEY

purposely
created
PUBLISHING

**MODERN-DAY STRATEGIES FOR
COMMUNITY ENGAGEMENT**

Published by Purposely Created Publishing Group™
Copyright © 2020 MaKara Rumley
All rights reserved.

Printed in the United States of America

ISBN: 978-1-64484-130-3

I dedicate this book to Earl and Darrilyn,
who have always been my head cheerleaders.
Thank you to Chace for coming up with the title
for the book. Thank you to Redd, who has always
been in my corner from day one. To my boys,
Robert and River, my moon and my sun!

TABLE OF CONTENTS

PREFACE

People always ask me why the name of my company is Hummingbird Firm. Well, the hummingbird is the only bird that can fly forward, backwards, and straight up. It is a colorful, petite, and agile bird possessing the nimbleness necessary to navigate tight quarters and changing conditions. The hummingbird represents community engagement at its best, in its purest form. The Hummingbird Firm patterns its approach after the bird's characteristics to maneuver situations. We know that the best laid plans and strategies can fail due to unforeseen changes in circumstances. It is crucial for community engagement professionals to move with the process, making accommodations for culture, historical context, political pressures, and identified priorities. At Hummingbird Firm, we strive to present the purest, sincerest effort and go beyond the expected, beyond the status quo, to achieve the ultimate goal of connecting with communities for our clients. Connecting with communities is *hard!* By using a cultural lens and proven strategies, companies and organizations can be successful.

INTRODUCTION

I began my matriculation at Spelman College as a math major, seeking to participate in the dual degree program and attend Georgia Tech University to earn an engineering degree. However, after attending a class taught by Dr. Robert Bullard, who is considered the godfather of environmental justice, I changed my major to sociology with a minor in political science. At the time, Dr. Bullard had published *Dumping in Dixie: Race, Class, and Environmental Quality*. I was immediately floored by the historic siting of pollution in poor black neighborhoods. Learning that Native American reservations also were dumping grounds for toxic waste and that there hadn't been much policy change in environmental siting, the book inspired me to develop solutions to change the paradigm. I decided to use law as my tool to intentionally address the disproportionate exposure of land, air, and water pollution on communities of color. I wanted to influence better decision making and help companies bridge the cultural gap between their projects and impacted communities. After completing law school and starting a family, I began to work as an environmental justice (EJ) attorney. At one point I was considered the only coined EJ attorney in the state of Georgia. Because there is no environmental justice law, it is necessary to use whatever tools you have at your disposal to mitigate exposure for communities. I used federal environmental statutes such as the Clean Air and Clean Water Act, lobbied elected officials, and used media campaigns to educate and disseminate information. I developed such a knack for communicating about large projects that impacted vulnerable communities that I was asked by the Environmental Protection Agency (EPA) Region 4 Administrator, Heather McTeer-Toney, to be her Senior Advisor on Community Engagement. Region 4 comprises North Carolina, South Carolina, Georgia, Alabama, Mississippi, Kentucky, Tennessee, Florida, and seven federally recognized Native American tribes. In that role, I traveled all over the Southeast and the nation looking at what was and wasn't working in communicating with communities. I was a master problem solver and would often be called upon to strategize about how to address challenges in connecting with impacted communities. Gina McCarthy, the EPA Administrator under the Obama Administration, had an initiative entitled "Making a Visible Difference in Communities." I led this initiative for Region 4, managing a team with representatives from each department and the Regional Administrator's office. Environmental projects take a very long time, and agencies usually only touch base with residents at the start and end of a project. Community members would tell me that they felt that there was a lack of transparency and that there were no visible successes. I learned that people need milestones that they can see, feel, and touch. If their senses can't validate that something is actually being accomplished, seeds of distrust and suspicion are planted. Also, when information is presented in an intimidating manner using unfamiliar terminology, residents often maintain a negative view of a project that could actually be improving their neighborhood. Often, an absence of people who look like them explaining complicated material breeds resentment and rejection. Once my tenure was over at the EPA, I decided to use the wisdom gleaned from these community conversations. They motivated me to found Hummingbird Firm, a company designed to bridge the divide between communities and large-scale projects. I created a place where engagement can take flight with all of the agility and nimbleness needed to adapt to challenges and reach prioritized goals. Hummingbird Firm ensures the success of projects by providing proven, measured community engagement services and products that build bridges between projects, people, and the "bottom-line." For our clients and partners, we effectively minimize headline risk (negative media stories), mitigate project delays, and create equitable results that foster goodwill amid diverse stakeholders. By elevating community priorities, we are able to cradle platforms for collaboration. Our clients include landscape design architects, engineering and infrastructure firms, public utilities, private developers, local and federal agencies, and non-profits. We specialize in community engagement and facilitation, strategic planning, and strategic communications with a niche in the environmental and transportation industry.

ALONE WE CAN DO SO LITTLE. TOGETHER WE CAN DO SO MUCH.

—Helen Keller

CHAPTER 1:

WHAT IS COMMUNITY ENGAGEMENT?

The aim of community engagement is to better mobilize a group of people to achieve long-term and resilient outcomes, processes, relationships, discourse, decision-making, and/or implementation. To be successful, it must be culturally competent, reflecting the community context in which it occurs. Community engagement is intricate, layered, and ever changing, which is why a range of tools and strategies must be employed to ensure success. The only way that it can be done effectively is if trust is fostered and/or enhanced. Trust is the critical element in long-term, sustainable engagement and effective governance. It is therefore a strategic process with the specific purpose of working with identified groups of people, whether they are connected by geographic location, special interest, or affiliation to identify and address issues affecting their wellbeing. The connection of the terms "community" to "engagement" can sometimes be misleading in that members of a community have many commonalities while simultaneously possessing points of contention. In practice, community engagement is a blend of science and skill—it's nuanced. The science comes from sociology, public policy, political science, cultural anthropology, organizational development, psychology, social psychology, and other disciplines. It also comes from organizing concepts drawn from the literature on community participation, community development, constituency building, and community psychology. The talent necessary to facilitate community engagement originates from the understanding and sensitivity used to apply and adapt the science in ways that fit the community and the purposes of specific collaboration efforts. The results of these activities may be defined differently and can encompass a broad range of structures (e.g., coalitions, partnerships, collaborations), but they all fall under the general rubric of community engagement and are treated similarly (adapted from Agency for Toxic Substances and Disease Registry [ATSDR], 2011). Community engagement can be complex, emotional, and labor intensive and requires dedicated resources such as time, funding, and people with the necessary skills. Citizens and leaders in communities across the United States, and indeed in many parts of the world, are struggling to make the right choices for the communities and issues they address. Building and implementing effective strategies requires a solid foundation in the best tools, techniques, and information available. The real challenge comes when there is a lack of understanding about what community engagement is and its importance throughout the lifespan of a project. Often this interaction is attempted after decisions are made, deposits have been paid, and contracts have been signed. Then comes backlash and rejection of a project that wasn't properly vetted by the people who actually live in the neighborhood where the project is set to take place. Companies, government, and organizations often attempt to do community engagement in-house because they think that a Power Point presentation followed by a question and answer session will suffice. They don't understand or respect the complexity and possible pitfalls of ill-prepared presentations and poorly timed meetings. As a result, developers, companies, and municipalities can be met with negative press, protests, a misinformed community, and/or be looked upon despairingly by the public at large. Engagement is *not* outreach; engagement is *not* involvement. These terms are often used interchangeably with "engagement" but do not share the same methodologies or goals. Engagement builds relationships to facilitate an exchange of information and feedback to inform reaching a mutually beneficial result. It remains the proactive step that makes the most sense when handling potentially controversial projects and projects located in underserved communities. Also, because of the skill necessary to lead effective community engagement, choosing consultants who do not have specific expertise in this discipline can prove detrimental to all. Sufficient resources and time must be allocated to achieve reliable results and reach a modicum of success.

CASE STUDY: PROCTOR CREEK (ATLANTA, GA)

The Environmental Protection Agency (EPA) Urban Waters Initiative, Proctor Creek, located in Atlanta, GA, is a clear case study for what community engagement is. Proctor Creek winds through downtown Atlanta and eventually connects to the Chattahoochee River. It passes through many vulnerable neighborhoods, which include some of the most marginalized groups (low-wealth, seniors, high-crime, food deserts, lack of transportation, health disparities, high crime). This waterway is plagued with pollution, erosion, and high bacteria levels from regular stormwater flooding and sewage overflows. In particular, the poor ecological health of this urban creek is attributed to illegal tire dumping/litter and combined and sanitary sewer overflows (CSO and SSO). The communities surrounding Proctor Creek suffer public health threats related to flooding and pathogens released from sewer overflow discharges. As new development and gentrification occurred, environmental justice issues became more prominent. The area is characterized by numerous brownfields (former industrial use properties) and little greenspace. Stakeholders in this community decided to work together; community groups and local residents help set up water quality monitoring, volunteer cleanup efforts, and coalitions to speak out about water quality concerns to community leaders. Through engagement, these communities presently pool efforts to ensure noticeable improvements. They decided to meet these challenges head on by coming together, engaging, and building partnerships with governments, NGOs, foundations, corporations, and academics. Leading with the rich history of the area, residents want to benefit from community improvements and increase their quality of life. As a result, they have been intentional about expressing their vision for themselves, advocating with elected officials for marked improvements, and often stepping outside of their comfort zone to build resiliency and lasting progress. The necessary improvements that this watershed needs is still a work in progress. However, with effective community engagement from all stakeholders, the goal of transforming this community will be reached. This is what community engagement is.

Have you witnessed community engagement in in your neighborhood?

_____

_____

_____

_____

_____

_____

_____

_____

_____

_____

_____

_____

_____

_____

_____

_____

_____

Have you been involved with a project that would have proved more successful if community engagement was activated?

_____

_____

_____

_____

_____

_____

_____

_____

_____

_____

_____

_____

_____

_____

_____

_____

_____

Have you witnessed a project that titled their interaction as community engagement, but participants didn't feel included in decision making?

_____

_____

_____

_____

_____

_____

_____

_____

_____

_____

_____

_____

_____

_____

_____

_____

_____

Use this page to write down your experiences and stories with projects in your neighborhood.

_____

_____

_____

_____

_____

_____

_____

_____

_____

_____

_____

_____

_____

_____

_____

_____

_____

_____

_____

Use this page to write down your experiences and stories with projects in your neighborhood.

_____

_____

_____

_____

_____

_____

_____

_____

_____

_____

_____

_____

_____

_____

_____

_____

_____

WE CANNOT LIVE ONLY
FOR OURSELVES.
A THOUSAND FIBERS CONNECT
US WITH OUR FELLOW MEN.

—Herman Melville

CHAPTER 2:

WHY BOTHER DOING COMMUNITY ENGAGEMENT?

We do community engagement because it is a way of ensuring that community members have direct involvement in decision making that impacts them, that they can contribute meaningfully in the decision-making processes, and that they develop functional capabilities that enable them to participate fully. When executed properly, it is the only way to bring a variety of stakeholders and impacted residents together to envision evolution for their neighborhoods. In turn, this approach ensures that decision makers are fully informed of all of the various viewpoints of a particular community and provides clarity on how the community sees themselves. Any improvements reached become sustainable because the community is invested in the success and can often become champions. If community engagement is not activated, the result is often strong opposition, project delays, and absence of good will. The private and public sector don't just activate community engagement because it's the morally right thing to do, they choose this communication methodology because it is the most straightforward way to ensure the success of a project. When community engagement is absent, resentment, anger, and distrust are often present. Organizations that want to get it right can't afford to not invest resources in this process.

CASE STUDY: PITTSBURGH COMMUNITY (ATLANTA, GA)

The Pittsburgh community was founded in the late 1800s by former slaves and has spent the last few decades attempting to combat foreclosures, mortgage fraud, flippers, vacant homes, and the various social ills—prostitution, drugs, squatters—that accompany real estate-downturned-impacted neighborhoods. In Pittsburgh, what was intended as an effort to bring art to an underserved community was instead considered an eyesore by some residents, specifically a group of ministers. The mural that was erected featured a big snake consuming a person. The response of Rev. Frank Brown of the Concerned Black Clergy, a well-connected coalition of Atlanta's African American ministers, to seeing this snake was, "When folks in this community see a big snake, the interpretation is that they see a serpent and the serpent represents Satan, and when you see images of dragons consuming people, it brings to mind the type of destruction the neighborhood was seeking to eliminate."

Other community members also felt strongly that a group of outsiders was imposing its idea of art on the neighborhood. Residents stated that they welcomed art in their neighborhood, but wished that they had been consulted regarding the type of art that was chosen. They didn't think that what was erected represented their community. LaShawn Hoffman of the Pittsburgh Community Improvement Association, which served as the de facto neighborhood association, stated that, "For some individuals in the neighborhood, it's the idea that, if we allow people to just continue to move in our neighborhood and do whatever, then we'll never be able to garner the community strength to pull ourselves up by our bootstraps to build a safer, vibrant, more thriving neighborhood." This conflict prompted City of Atlanta Councilwoman Joyce Shepherd to become involved. She sought to introduce legislation requiring artists seeking to paint murals to first be presented to the community. She also posed the following questions: How do we use this event to unite us as a community, not divide us? How do we start working through those other barriers that this incident brought up? How do we bring people to our neighborhood? How do we get people to respect our neighborhood? More importantly, how do we unite communities? In response, The Living Walls organization expressed that the incident convinced them to revise the process they used to select sites and reach out to the community. The lesson learned was that without having a conversation about what art means for a particular community, there will predictably be opposition when the proposed project isn't culturally competent. This story is a great example of *why* we do community engagement. This conflict could have been avoided if the community had simply been engaged at the beginning of the process. Living Walls should have researched the history of the neighborhood and cultural norms and made an effort to understand the people who would be viewing the mural on a daily basis.

Do you have a business case for community engagement?

_____

_____

_____

_____

_____

_____

_____

_____

_____

_____

_____

_____

_____

_____

_____

_____

_____

_____

_____

_____

Will community engagement save you time, money, and misunderstandings?

Use this page to write down your experiences and stories with projects in your neighborhood.

_____

_____

_____

_____

_____

_____

_____

_____

_____

_____

_____

_____

_____

_____

_____

_____

_____

Use this page to write down your experiences and stories with projects in your neighborhood.

_____

_____

_____

_____

_____

_____

_____

_____

_____

_____

_____

_____

_____

_____

_____

_____

_____

_____

Use this page to write down your experiences and stories with projects in your neighborhood.

_____

_____

_____

_____

_____

_____

_____

_____

_____

_____

_____

_____

_____

_____

_____

_____

_____

_____

IF YOU WANT TO GO QUICKLY, GO ALONE. IF YOU WANT TO GO FAR, GO TOGETHER.

—African Proverb

CHAPTER 3:

WITH WHOM DO YOU ENGAGE?

The word "community" is a broad term used to define groups of people, whether they are stakeholders, interest groups, or citizen groups. A community may be a geographic location (community of place), a people united by similar interests (community of practice), or people united by affiliation or identity, such as an industry. Local businesses, elected officials, churches, schools, senior centers, recreation centers, and neighborhood groups are examples of who can compose one community. Depending on the project or initiative, it is necessary to tailor your prioritized audience. For example, erecting a park might glean the most interest from houses close by, families with children, and schools, while building a road that requires the tearing down of houses would garner attention from the residents of the homes impacted, surrounding houses in the neighborhood, and elected officials. Often, there is a mix of resident homeowners and absentee landowners.

Depending on the type of project, it may be necessary to determine how to connect with both effectively. There may also be different neighborhoods within a given community that possess differing characteristics and priorities. One neighborhood could have a high senior population and highly educated retirees while another could have a more transient natured population composed of young children, where multiple languages are spoken. It is necessary to do a walking and windshield tour to determine how your prioritized community is arranged. Windshield tours are observations made from a moving vehicle. Walking tours are observations made on foot. Either or both can help you better understand either the community in general or a specific condition or aspect of it. In order to be truly culturally competent in your engagement, either or both of these information gathering approaches should be used. Windshield surveys are particularly useful when the area you want to observe is large and the aspects you're interested in can be seen from the road. A walking survey might be a better choice when you're seeking to understand things that are harder to see from a moving vehicle, such as noise level, resident activity during different times of the day, and conversations.

Windshield and walking surveys can be used to assess general community needs–to estimate the poverty level, for example–or to examine more specific facets of the community's physical, social, or economic character. Some possible assessment qualities include:

- Housing stock
- Infrastructure needs
- The viability of businesses and industrial facilities
- The presence or absence of public spaces
- The amount of activity on the streets at various times of the day, week, or year
- The noise level in various parts of the community
- The amount and movement of traffic at various times of day
- The location and condition of public buildings, e.g. the city or town hall or courthouse

On a granular level, one can assess where the hubs of communication are located to better connect with community members in the spaces where they feel most comfortable and safe.

CASE STUDY: TURKEY CREEK GREENWAY PROJECT (GULFPORT, MS)

In 1866, a group of recently emancipated African Americans settled on the banks of Turkey Creek, where they founded a new community. It seemed like a great location to settle because they were close to an inexhaustible supply of clean water that they could use for everything from drinking to bathing to baptisms. For more than one hundred years, Turkey Creek's settlers and their descendants thrived, forming a tight-knit and self-sufficient Mississippi Gulf Coast community that developed and maintained its own distinct cultural heritage. In recent decades, many forms of outside pollution, including acidification, fecal coliform, and dioxin contamination from a variety of sources, have compromised and plagued the area around the Turkey Creek Watershed. In addition, it was not just the slave descendants whose impact needed to be considered, but also the very significant Vietnamese American community as well. Many Vietnamese Americans settled in the Mississippi Gulf area, bringing their fishing traditions over from their home country. It was important that their viewpoints were considered in the vision for an improved watershed. Thao Vu, Executive Director of Mississippi Coalition for Vietnamese-American Fisher Folks and Families, expressed that community engagement must account for diverse needs, such as translation services. "Large climate events and flooding impact not just their homes, but also their fishing infrastructure—their livelihoods. Future disasters only exacerbate [the] losses and impacts they've experienced. FEMA aid centers set up after Katrina did not have adequate translators or materials written in a manner people [could] understand. Title VI of the Civil Rights Act and executive order[s] should address diversity of language in the community, but we do not have a model of compliance here in Mississippi." In truly connecting with that community in the Turkey Creek Watershed, language translation and concerns about jobs had to be addressed. This is a great example of a segmented community, unifying to partner with a coalition of federal, state, and local groups to restore the now environmentally challenged watershed. That coalition has made significant progress, including:

- In 2004, EPA awarded a $150,000 Clean Water Act (CWA) grant to the Land Trust for the Mississippi Coastal Plain (LTMCP) to build watershed partnerships in six watersheds, including Turkey Creek.

- In 2006, a locally led multi-stakeholder watershed team of 15 local, state, and federal organizations developed and began using a watershed plan to clean up existing pollution and build a proposed 1,000-acre greenway in the community.

- In August 2007, residents were successful in getting the state of Mississippi to upgrade the water quality criteria for Turkey Creek from secondary contact recreation, such as boating and other activities where incidental contact with the water may occur, to primary contact recreation, which incorporates baptismal rites as an existing use.

- As of 2010, LTMCP acquired 400 acres of greenway using land donated by the city of Gulfport, local landowners and a $425,000 grant from Mississippi Department of Equality.

- In 2015, The National Fish and Wildlife Foundation awarded $7.5M to the Mississippi Department of Environmental Quality to conserve important habitat and enhance water quality in the 30,000- acre Turkey Creek watershed through habitat and stream conservation and restoration. (https://www.mdeq.ms.gov/wp-content/uploads/2017/09/Habitat-Restoration-and-Conservation-in-Turkey-Creek-Phase-I.pdf)

- In 2016, Urban Waters Research Project, Anacostia Community Documentation Initiative, listened to the stories of what these communities struggle with and witnessed their coalition building. The researcher, Susana Raab, was reminded about how fragile history is, the depth of human suffering, and the power and necessity of partnership in speaking truth to power. It is through recording and disseminating stories like those of Turkey Creek and the Gulf Coast that the Anacostia Community Museum sought to share and store history and culture for the betterment of communities in the future.

- In 2018, EPA awarded $25K to Mississippi State University for Rural Voices Radio: Voices Along the Gulf. The Mississippi Writing/Thinking Institute at Mississippi State University (MSU) worked with students to develop environmental content for Rural Voices Radio: Voices Along the Gulf. The award supported two school groups, Bay-Waveland Middle School in Bay St. Louis and Stone High School in Wiggins, and one non-profit organization, the Hancock County Historical Society.

- In order to build on these successes and continue to improve community life around Turkey Creek, coalitions continue to monitor water quality and create more public access through the construction of a series of boardwalks, natural areas, and hiking and walking trails. While there has been a concerted effort to search out sources of pollution and find ways to abate their impacts via highly technical means, the story of the watershed and the residents' connection to the water has been an essential part of the restoration effort.

- This is with *whom* you engage. By bringing stakeholder groups into the fold, lasting progress and resilience can be achieved.

What groups make up your community?

_____

_____

_____

_____

_____

_____

_____

_____

_____

_____

_____

_____

_____

_____

_____

_____

_____

_____

How many languages are spoken in your community?

Describe an example in your neighborhood when groups were stronger together than apart.

_____

_____

_____

_____

_____

_____

_____

_____

_____

_____

_____

_____

_____

_____

_____

_____

_____

_____

Use this page to write down your experiences and stories with projects in your neighborhood.

_____

_____

_____

_____

_____

_____

_____

_____

_____

_____

_____

_____

_____

_____

_____

_____

_____

_____

_____

Use this page to write down your experiences and stories with projects in your neighborhood.

_____

_____

_____

_____

_____

_____

_____

_____

_____

_____

_____

_____

_____

_____

_____

_____

YOU CANNOT BUY ENGAGEMENT. YOU HAVE TO BUILD ENGAGEMENTS.

—Tara Nicholle-Nelson

CHAPTER 4:

HOW DO YOU DO COMMUNITY ENGAGEMENT?

The ethos that "we are stronger together" often leads the strategic approach when introducing a new project to a group of stakeholders. The purpose of government, companies, and non-profits investing in this type of process is to establish trust. Once trust is solidified, discussions contain less animosity and disdain and collaboration and clear communication can occur. When gathering those that are interested in a particular initiative, here are some approaches on how to activate networks.

Cultural Competency

Cultural competence is the ability to understand, communicate with, and eff ectively interact with people across cultures. Culture is defined as the customs, arts, social institutions, and achievements of a particular nation, people, or other social group. Many professionals miss that a particular culture is present for subgroups too, such as rock climbers, runners, and cyclists. Neighborhoods contain a myriad of cultures living in a particular square-mile radius. Culture can also be industry specific, such as engineers, attorneys, and geologists. A cultural competency analysis is an essential component when developing a community engagement plan. It sets the framework for authentic and respectful interactions, establishing trust with the community and stakeholders alike. Cultural competence is the ability to interact effectively with people of different cultures and helps ensure that the needs of all community members are addressed. In practice, both individuals and organizations can be culturally competent. Culture must be considered at every step of the way because it goes beyond just race or ethnicity. It can also refer to such characteristics as age, gender, sexual orientation, disability, religion, income level, education, geographical location, or profession. Cultural competence means to be respectful and responsive to the health beliefs and practices—and cultural and linguistic needs—of diverse population groups. Developing cultural competence is also an evolving, dynamic process that takes time and occurs along a continuum. Practicing cultural competence throughout the planning process ensures that all members of a community are represented and included. It can also prevent wasteful spending and ineffective approaches that could alienate instead of connect with prioritized communities. We use the following tactics to incorporate cultural competence in our engagement process:

1. Ensure community involvement in all steps, where permitted

2. Use a population-based definition of community (let the community define itself)

3. Stress the importance of relevant, culturally appropriate engagement approaches

4. Employ culturally competent evaluators (make sure some of the evaluators look like the communities in question)

Engagement Tactics

A variety of outreach tactics can be used, including but not limited to public meetings, one-on-ones, charrettes (a meeting in which all stakeholders in a project attempt to resolve conflicts and map solutions), community meetings, listening sessions, and interviews. For digitally minded audiences, regardless of race or income, a strong social media presence is key. It may be necessary to recalibrate tactics according to who you want to reach. For some community members, there may be a strong focus on Twitter and Instagram, whereas for others, Facebook will be more effective. Establishing a leadership team of citizens and others who can convene meetings to articulate values, determine roles, and create working agreements on behalf of community interests can often be helpful. This team would generally help ensure a community-driven process that shapes positive and equitable project outcomes.

Community Investment

Giving stipends to community members who assist with planning and executing community outreach in their neighborhoods is a tried and true step to community buy-in and relationship building. Compensating residents acknowledges that their time and input are valued and it is an organic way to invest in the success of the project.

Equitable Storytelling

Advance narratives that undo stereotypes and contribute to justice, solidarity and healing by allowing community members to speak for themselves and tell their own stories. Story mapping collaboratively with communities often highlights their cultural history.

CASE STUDY: ARCGIS STORYMAPS PROCTOR CREEK WATERSHED (ATLANTA, GA)

ArcGIS StoryMaps is a tool that anyone can use to tell remarkable stories with custom maps that inform and inspire. A story can effect change, influence opinion, and create awareness, and maps are an integral part of storytelling. ArcGIS StoryMaps gives community narratives a stronger sense of place, illustrates spatial relationships, and adds visual appeal and credibility to projects. Proctor Creek Watershed used this tool in collaboration with EPA Region 4 to clearly illustrate their story and the location of environmental challenges. The map has tabs for the issue, background/history, key groups/organizations, demographics, strategies for solutions, and outcomes. By using this tool, which was populated with information obtained in collaboration with the community, anyone can learn the past, present, and future of the watershed.

For clarity, StoryMaps are usually funded by government entities to gain community context, build relationships with stakeholders, and establish trust. There are numerous examples of maps created by local municipalities and federal agencies.

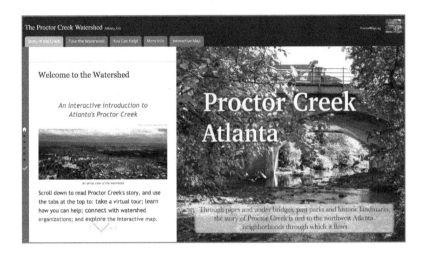

How could you use maps and storytelling to better connect with your community?

_____

_____

_____

_____

_____

_____

_____

_____

_____

_____

_____

_____

_____

_____

_____

_____

_____

_____

_____

_____

Are there stories that need to be told about the history of your neighborhood?

Is there neighborhood context that could better inform project decisions?

_____

_____

_____

_____

_____

_____

_____

_____

_____

_____

_____

_____

_____

_____

_____

_____

Does your community participate in a visioning plan? If no, how would you like for your community to improve?

_____

_____

_____

_____

_____

_____

_____

_____

_____

_____

_____

_____

_____

_____

_____

_____

_____

What about your community makes you proud?

_____

_____

_____

_____

_____

_____

_____

_____

_____

_____

_____

_____

_____

_____

_____

_____

_____

_____

DON'T BUILD LINKS.
BUILD RELATIONSHIPS.

—Rand Fishkin

CHAPTER 5:

WHERE DO YOU CONDUCT COMMUNITY ENGAGEMENT?

Meetings

In-person meetings and engagement activities should begin with expectation setting so that each participant understands the goal of the interaction and the benefit to everyone in attendance. For each event that is scheduled to last more than one hour, community engagement professionals should work to ensure the following:

Timing

Choose times of day that are convenient for people who work 9am-5pm shifts. For those who work the third shift or irregular hours, provide robust alternatives to in-person engagement.

Transportation

Host meetings in areas that are accessible by public transport, have free parking, are in well-lit areas, and in spaces that are in close proximity to major walkable residential areas.

Childcare

Seek to ensure that spaces will feature a separate child engagement area so that parents/grandparents/legal guardians can actively participate without distractions.

Equity

For vulnerable communities that cannot devote time to multiple meetings/sessions or are excluded based on jargon alone, engagement strategies should include shorter, more intimate engagement sessions. For those meetings, it is recommended that spaces that feel more like a living room than a conference room be identified. Look for warm colors versus sterile environments or places where you can take your shoes off and sit cross-legged on the floor.

At Hummingbird Firm, we like to incorporate modern-day communication tools, such as geofencing, message-to-text, online surveys, and story maps. Regular updates to interested stakeholders are integral to maintaining relationships and trust.

CASE STUDY: GEORGIA STAND-UP AND MARTA (ATLANTA, GA)

Georgia Strategic Alliance for New Directions and Unified Policies (Georgia STAND-UP), is a think and act tank for working communities. This Georgia alliance of leaders represents community, faith, academic, and labor organizations that organize and educate communities about issues related to economic development. Georgia STAND-UP and MARTA, the public transit system in Atlanta, GA, teamed up to engage with underserved communities for the "More MARTA" initiative. MARTA wanted to get feedback from riders at its Oakland City, West End, Five Points, and Georgia State stations. Because Georgia STAND-UP had a strong reputation for effectively engaging with people who lived around those stations, a partnership was formed to help conduct surveys. More MARTA staff and volunteers were only anticipating roughly 20 completed surveys per station, per day, but Georgia STAND-UP's approach produced results that far exceeded those expectations. They were able to successfully complete over 500 surveys between the two days of More MARTA surveying and the Community Conversation event. They handed out swag bags and roundtrip MARTA fare to incentivize riders to participate. By meeting riders where they were–at the station that they frequent–they were able to garner more participation than if they just had a community meeting. It is important to determine which tactics will work best based off cultural competency. The surveyors looked like the riders, which made them more receptive to being approached for a conversation. Additionally, modern technology (tablets) was used to complete the surveys. They also used video to record feedback. Finally, they chose a time of day when they would connect the most with riders. The surveyors were pleasant, personable, engaging, and had positive attitudes. At the Community Conversation event held at West End Mall, there were over 100 people in attendance who voiced their concerns. They asked questions about fund allocations, requested necessities at stations with the highest ridership, such as open restrooms, fixed elevators, and escalators. The riders wanted safer stations with more security and cleanliness. This event was also attended by then Assistant General Manager, Ben Limmer, who stayed to hear community concerns and answer questions. His presence was essential, as it represented MARTA's willingness to create a better experience for that community. By partnering with community engagement experts, MARTA was able to effectively connect, communicate, and engage.

WE ARE WHAT WE REPEATEDLY DO. EXCELLENCE THEN IS NOT AN ACT, BUT A HABIT

—Aristotle

CHAPTER 6:

ENGAGEMENT TOOLS

Technology

<u>Website</u>: Having a mobile-friendly website that houses the information for a particular project is helpful. There are many people who still don't have computers, but those same people do have a smartphone, which allows them to access information.

<u>Online Engagement Software</u>: There are many software tools that community engagement professionals use to track engagement. If engagement isn't tracked and measured, then there can be no determination that the chosen tools and tactics are effective.

<u>Message to Text</u>: There are so many bounce-backs from email communications, and often your email can end up in someone's spam box, never to be seen. A modern communication tool is message to text. Most everyone will open a text message. Include a link to the website and capture the attention of more people.

Geofencing: It is possible to draw a digital fence around a specific neighborhood. By taking advantage of the unique code on each person's mobile device that has enabled location services, companies can advertise information about upcoming public meetings and other engagement opportunities.

Livestreaming: Not everyone can attend in-person events due to conflicts with their job or family obligations. However, if you livestream meetings, those same people can participate and engage from anywhere.

Media

Social: Segment the community and choose the social media platform that they use the most. Demographic data can be very helpful in making these choices.

Traditional: Printed information is still helpful for the senior population and connecting with people during walking tours of a neighborhood.

Meetings

Public: These are usually large meetings that present information and provide opportunities for questions and in-person engagement.

Focus Groups: These are segmented groups of the community; you can ask them a series of specific questions and get feedback on scenarios created to gather information about their perspectives.

<u>Charrettes</u>: These are usually interactive meetings where participants can look at blown-up maps or options for development and give suggestions on what needs to be changed or enhanced.

<u>One-on-One Interviews</u>: Sometimes it is best to talk to thought leaders and elected officials directly to gather their perspectives.

<u>Surveys</u>: Usually a list of questions that elicit thought-provoking feedback and contextual perspectives. These can be conducted in person and via electronic and digital platforms.

<u>Pop-Ups</u>: You set up shop where your prioritized communities naturally interact, such as the grocery story, sports events, and festivals.

5 STEPS FOR MAKING SURE PEOPLE SHOW UP TO YOUR MEETING

Timing

Choose times of day that are convenient for people who work 9am - 5pm shifts as well as irregular hour shifts. Also, using live streaming can expand participation for those who can't attend in person.

Transportation

Host meetings in areas that are accessible by public transit, have free parking, and are in well-lit areas. Select locations that are in close proximity to major walkable residential areas.

Childcare

Don't exclude people who are interested by not having childcare. Have a separate child engagement area so that parents/ grandparents/ legal guardians can actively engage without distraction.

Food

People are more attentive with full bellies. Have water, coffee, snacks or a hot meal (buffet style) if during dinner time. Also, food always serves as an incentive for people to attend.

Equity

Not all people can devote time to multiple meetings. And sometimes jargon alone makes people feel excluded. Create shorter more intimate settings, steer clear of sterile environments, and use plain language.

www.hummingbirdfirm.com

74

Worksheet 1: Stakeholder Identification
Use this worksheet and the accompanying exercise to identify stakeholders to include in the planning process.

Instructions: 1) Identify the broad topic or specific issues to be addressed by planning.
2) Identify types of stakeholders potentially interested in or affected by the issue.
3) Identify specific individuals or groups that should be involved.

Identify Potential Stakeholders	Identify Potential Issues				
	Example Transportation	Economic Development	Housing	Agriculture	Natural Resources
Example Local Government • Elected officials • Local departments • Regional government • State government • Federal government • Quasi-public agencies	Public works Highway dept Planning dept RPC / Metro planning org DOT	Community development Econ dev corporation Chamber of commerce WEDC	Housing authority WHEDA HUD	Land and water conservation Extension DATCP	Parks and recreation Land and water conservation DNR
Community Members • Age • Gender • Race/ethnicity • Income/employment • Housing status • Familial status • Geographic location • Political view • Opinion leaders					
Organizations • Civic • Cultural • Religious • Business • Geographic • Special Interest					
Private Sector • Health • Education • Business • Retail/services • Manufacturing • Construction • Agriculture • Forestry • Other					

Exercise 1: Stakeholder Relationship Mapping
Use the following space or a large sheet of paper to identify stakeholders and their relationships to local planning issues and/or each other. If desired, make notes directly on the paper or use different symbols or lines to identify important relationships (i.e. common interests, influence, etc.). This type of exercise is useful for identifying stakeholders, brainstorming potential issues, and uncovering hidden relationships.

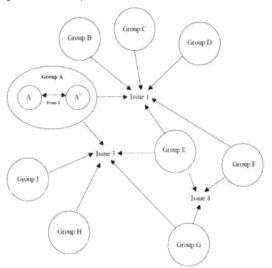

Examples:

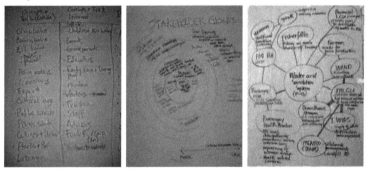

Graphic from Bryson, 2004 and Bryant, 2003. Photos 1 and 2 from Stakeholder Analysis, Museum Notes Blog, February 7, 2011. Photo 3 from Stakeholder Interests, Sustainable Sanitation and Water Management, 2010.

Modern-Day Strategies for Community Engagement

Worksheet 2: Stakeholder Analysis
Use this worksheet and the accompanying exercise to analyze important stakeholder characteristics and begin to identify a strategy for involvement.

Instructions: 1) Make a list of potential stakeholders (see Worksheet 1).
2) Note how each stakeholder is interested in, able to influence, and likely to participate in the process. Describe additional characteristics as needed.

List Potential Stakeholders	Goals, motivations and interests	Power and influence	Knowledge, resources and support
Example Citizens for a greener tomorrow	Interested in preserving urban biodiversity by establishing a network of trails and open space.	No official power but able to influence and inform a large number of members.	Knowledgeable and supportive of previous planning efforts. Able to provide volunteers.

Exercise 2: Stakeholder Analysis Matrix
Use the following space or a large sheet of paper to identify and classify stakeholders according to selected dimensions. Represent one stakeholder dimension along each axis. If desired, use different symbols, colors, sizes or lines to represent a third dimension (i.e. size of symbol = degree of influence). Begin to make note of potential strategies to involve each group. This type of exercise is useful for analyzing how stakeholders relate to an issue or process, and identifying methods to engage stakeholders.

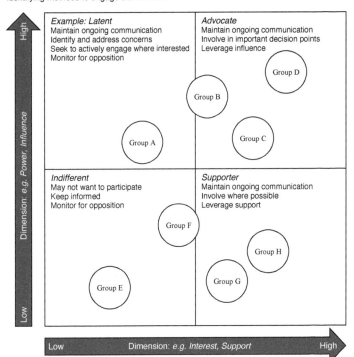

Stakeholder Dimensions:

Power: the power a stakeholder has over the decision
Influence: the ability of a stakeholder to influence other stakeholders
Impact: the degree to which the decision will impact each stakeholder
Interest: the perceived level of interest that each stakeholder has in the decision
Support: the degree to which a stakeholder supports or opposes the project
Resources: the level of resources a stakeholder is able to bring to the process
Knowledge: the level of knowledge a stakeholder has about the project

Adapted from *Tools for Institutional, Political and Social Analysis of Policy Reform: Annex.* 2007. The World Bank.

Worksheet 3: Public Participation Strategy
Use this worksheet to develop a strategy for public participation, including methods, timing and audience.

Instructions:
1) Identify tasks to complete during each major step of the planning process.
2) Identify objectives for public participation at various points in the process.
3) Identify tools and stakeholders appropriate for each task.

Identify Planning Tasks	Identify Participation Strategy				
Example	Awareness	Education	Input	Interaction	Decision
Data Collection and Analysis	✓	✓	✓		
1. Identify data and information needs			Plan commission		
2. Gather spatial and technical data					
3. Verify data for accuracy			Data review committee of citizen/experts		
4. Analyze data for patterns and trends					
5. Disseminate information	Press release targeting general public	Kickoff mtg. targeting general public			
Issue Identification					
1.					
2.					
3.					
Goal and Objective Formulation					
1.					
2.					
3.					
Strategy Formulation					
1.					
2.					
3.					
Plan Review and Approval					
1.					
2.					
3.					

Adapted from *Crafting an Effective Plan for Public Participation*, Miskowiak, 2004. Center for Land Use Education.

MaKara Rumley

Worksheet 4: Barriers to Participation
Use this worksheet to refine the public participation strategy by identifying barriers to participation and potential solutions.

Instructions: 1) Identify barriers to participation based on knowledge of stakeholders (Worksheets 1 and 2) and previous participation experience (Worksheet 7).
2) Identify potential solutions, noting audience, timing and methods as appropriate.

Barriers	Solution
Example Geography - woodland and lakefront property owners live outside of region	• Send survey and mailings to permanent residence • Hold weekend meetings during prime visitor season • Provide webinars to capture those unable to travel • Post all relevant project information on website
Transportation	
Language or reading skills	
Cultural or ethnic sensitivities	
Political sensitivities	
Family/work obligations	
Level of interest	

80

Worksheet 5: Communication Strategy
Use this worksheet to develop a communication strategy for public participation, including key information to relay to the public and preferred techniques.

Event: _____

Participation objective: _____

Target audience: _____

Date: _____ Time: _____

Key Information	Responsible party	Target completion
Identify the key information you will relay to the public.		

Technical Information	Responsible party	Target completion
Identify technical and background information needed to ensure meaningful participation.		

Communication Techniques	Responsible party	Target completion
Identify techniques to communicate with the public.		

❑ Public notice (posting, newspaper, etc.)

❑ Mass media (press release, letter to the editor, interview, etc.)

❑ Internet (email, calendar of events, Facebook, etc.)

❑ Print (postcard, factsheet, handout, etc.)

❑ Display (poster, map, photos, scale model, etc.)

❑ Audiovisual (PowerPoint presentation, video, etc.)

❑ Other:

Worksheet 6: Event Logistics
Use this worksheet to plan for individual public participation events, including facility, room setup and equipment needs.

Event: _____

Participation objective: _____

Target audience: _____

Date: _____ Time: _____

Facility	Responsible party	Target completion

Name: _____

Location: _____

Contact person: _____

Phone: _____ Email: _____

Rental fee: _____ Capacity: _____

Features: ❏ Adequate parking ❏ Restrooms ❏ Handicap accessible ❏ Other: _____

Equipment	Responsible party	Target completion

❏ Directional signage

❏ Name tags

❏ Sign-in sheet

❏ Presentation materials (maps, posters, PowerPoint presentation, etc.)

❏ Facilitation materials (flipchart, markers, paper, pens, post-it notes, sticky dots, etc.)

❏ A/V equipment (laptop, projector, screen, cart, extension cord, microphone, speakers, etc.)

❏ Refreshments (food, beverages, serving ware, tablecloth, waste/recycling, etc.)

❏ Handouts

❏ Evaluation forms

Room Setup	Responsible party	Target completion

❏ Tables: (registration, refreshments, handouts, displays, etc.)

❏ Chairs:

❏ Other:

❏ Room arrangement:

The physical arrangement of a room sets the tone for public participation. Use the following diagrams to select an arrangement that is appropriate for the intended event. Consider the number of participants, level of interaction and meeting goals.

Circle

A plain circle of chairs is useful when the full involvement of each individual is required. This arrangement encourages discussion and interaction among peers and downplays the role of the leader. Use of audiovisuals or a flip chart may be difficult. If needed, tables can be used to remove the sense of vulnerability some participants may experience. Ideal for up to 20 participants.

Conference Table

Ideal for small groups where close interaction and a lot of discussion are expected. Sharing a single table creates unity but may also suggest formality or hierarchy. Most effective with groups of 6-15 where participants can see and hear each other easily. If the group gets too large, people at the far end of the table may feel left out and form a separate group. Participants may need to move their chairs to properly view a presentation.

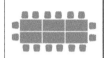

U-Shape

Popular set-up for groups where close interaction or collaboration is necessary. Gives participants a sense that they are equal in status. Group size should be limited to about 20 people so that participants can easily see and hear each other. Front area can be used for audiovisuals and center area for simulations or role plays. A table could be added to the front of this arrangement to create additional seating, but may limit functionality.

Classroom

A classroom-style setup provides a work surface for note taking and reference materials. It is ideal for one-way communication such as audiovisual presentations and lecture style programs. Though not ideal, participants can also break out into small groups at their tables or turn to the table behind them. Visibility and group interaction can be enhanced by arranging furniture in a semi-circle. Sound amplification may be needed in larger rooms.

Banquet

Ideal for small group discussion and project work within a larger group setting. Participants are seated at round or small rectangular tables. To maximize visibility, tables can be arranged in a semi-circle and seating limited to one side of the table. Small groups can easily return to the large group to focus on a speaker or audiovisual presentation. Sound amplification may be needed in larger rooms. A meal can be easily incorporated into this setup.

Theater

Ideal for one-way communication to large groups. Examples include audiovisual presentations and lecture style programs. Visibility can be enhanced by providing tiered seating or by placing chairs in a semi-circle. Note taking is cumbersome without tables. Sound amplification may be needed in larger rooms. Microphones placed throughout the room can be less intimidating than requiring speakers to come to the front of the room to provide input.

Worksheet 7: Event Debrief
Use this worksheet to evaluate the strengths and weaknesses of individual public participation events and transfer lessons to future activities.

Event: _____

Participation objective: _____

Target audience: _____

Date: _____ Time: _____

Strengths

What worked well? (timing, location, venue, activities, etc.)
- For specific audiences
- To achieve specific objectives

Weaknesses

What could have been improved?
- Barriers to participation
- Unanticipated events

Lessons Learned

What key learning experiences should be transferred to future events?

Worksheet 8: Documentation and Evaluation
Use this worksheet to document resources invested in the public participation program and evaluate its overall success.

Inputs: Document and evaluate resources invested in public participation		
Resources *Example* • Time • Money • Equipment • Technology • Staff • Volunteers • Partners	Evaluation Questions • Were sufficient resources allocated to the public participation program? What else was needed? • Did the results justify the costs?	Evaluation Results

Outputs: Document and evaluate public participation activities and involvement		
Activities • Notices • Educational materials • Meetings • Small group activities	Evaluation Questions • Were there a range of opportunities to participate, both in-person and remotely? • Were the locations convenient and accessible? • Was the information distributed clear and easy to understand? Was it timely?	Evaluation Results
Involvement • Number of participants • Diversity of participants • Attainment of objectives • Quality of input • Public satisfaction		

Outcomes: Document and evaluate short, medium and long-term results of public participation		
Short-term results • Increase knowledge • Obtain feedback • Resolve conflicts • Gain consensus • Influence decision-making	Evaluation Questions	Evaluation Results
Medium-term results • Adopt plan • Create policies, programs • Change behavior		
Long-term impacts • Change social conditions • Change economic conditions • Change environmental conditions		

Logic Model adapted from University of Wisconsin Cooperative Extension, Program Development and Evaluation.
www.uwex.edu/ces/pdande/evaluation/evallogicmodel.html

What partnerships will you form to increase the quality of life in your community?

_____

_____

_____

_____

_____

_____

_____

_____

_____

_____

_____

_____

_____

_____

_____

_____

What resources can you use to make sure that your community is involved in decision making that impacts their quality of life?

_____

_____

_____

_____

_____

_____

_____

_____

_____

_____

_____

_____

_____

_____

_____

_____

_____

Is there a neighborhood association or community groups that can serve as an advocate for residents?

_____

_____

_____

_____

_____

_____

_____

_____

_____

_____

_____

_____

_____

_____

_____

Does your community have the capacity to participate and form relationships with government and private industry?

_____

_____

_____

_____

_____

_____

_____

_____

_____

_____

_____

_____

_____

_____

_____

If you are a community engagement professional, what new approaches can you use to better connect with those impacted by the project that you are tasked with communicating about?

_____

_____

_____

_____

_____

_____

_____

_____

_____

_____

_____

_____

_____

_____

_____

_____

CONCLUSION

Community engagement is an invaluable, proactive, solution-oriented, and transformational endeavor that benefits all stakeholders. Government, companies, and non-profits can continue to utilize this approach to ensure successful, fully informed projects and initiatives. Hummingbird Firm was founded to be the connective tissue between large-scale projects and impacted communities. We serve as the translator for divergent viewpoints, building bridges between people and the "bottom line."

Beyond the Status Quo

Our interdisciplinary team and intentional partnering allow us to provide creative and innovative approaches to traditional goals.

Beyond the Expected

Our clients range from nonprofits to federal government agencies. We tailor our strategies to the unique needs of our clients and their goals. We identify, assess, and push beyond what our clients expect, always looking for ways to anticipate and surpass their requested deliverables.

REFERENCES

Chapter 1

"Principles of Community Engagement: First Edition," *Centers for Disease Control and Prevention: CDC/ATSDR Committee on Community Engagement*, 1997.

Chapter 2

Thomas Wheatley, "Living Walls Splits Community," *Creative Loafing*, November 14, 2012, https://creativeloafing. com/content-170659-Living-Walls-splits-community.

Chapter 3

"Surviving and Thriving in the Face of Rising Seas," Union of Concerned Scientists, November 2015, https://www.ucsusa.org/sites/default/files/attach/2015/11/surviving-and-thriving-executive-summary.pdf.

ABOUT THE AUTHOR

MaKara Rumley, Esq., is an experienced community engagement strategist and thought leader on cultural competence, equity, facilitation, stakeholder engagement, and measuring success. As the founder and chief engagement officer of Hummingbird Firm, a community engagement consulting company, she advises the public and private sectors on public involvement strategies that work. She has received numerous awards and recognitions in her field.

MaKara got her start as an environmental justice attorney, developing strategies to mitigate the disproportionate exposure of vulnerable and overburdened communities to land, air, and water pollution. She then served as a political appointee under the Obama administration in Region 4 of the Environmental Protection Agency as a Senior Advisor on Community Engagement. She is a board member at the Southface Institute and Piedmont Park Conservancy, an advisory board member of the Trust for Public Land Georgia, and serves on the Advisory Council of Advocates for The

King Center. MaKara is a proud graduate of Spelman College and the George Washington University Law School.

MaKara lives in Atlanta, Georgia, with her husband, three children, and dog. In her free time, she enjoys spending time with her family, traveling, crafting, and playing tennis.

To learn more, visit
www.hummingbirdfirm.com

CREATING DISTINCTIVE BOOKS
WITH INTENTIONAL RESULTS

We're a collaborative group of creative masterminds
with a mission to produce high-quality books to position
you for monumental success in the marketplace.

Our professional team of writers, editors, designers,
and marketing strategists work closely together to ensure
that every detail of your book is a clear representation
of the message in your writing.

Want to know more?
Write to us at info@publishyourgift.com
or call (888) 949-6228

Discover great books, exclusive offers, and more at
www.PublishYourGift.com

Connect with us on social media

@publishyourgift

CPSIA information can be obtained
at www.ICGtesting.com
Printed in the USA
BVHW020901031022
648542BV00020B/644

9 781644 841303